When Dad Scored a Goal in the Garden

Compiled by John Foster

Illustrated by Emi Ordás, Clare Elsom, Agnese Baruzzi,
Yannick Robert, Robin Boyden, Laura Ellen Anderson,
Lee Cosgrove and Olga Demidova

OXFORD
UNIVERSITY PRESS

Contents

Please Can I Have My Football Back?

Please can I have my football back?
You can pass it through the window.
It'll fit through the crack.
Please can I have my football back?

John Foster

Is this your football I found in my garden?

Is anything broken?

No.

Then it's mine.

Here Comes Ronaldo

Dad charged down the garden
With the ball at his feet.
'Here comes Ronaldo,' he cried,
'With just the goalie to beat.
He's round the keeper. It's an open goal.
He must score,' he said.
But he trod on the ball and fell
Head over heels into the flower bed!

Pam Johnson

I Dreamed I Scored for England

I dreamed I scored for England
And the crowd chanted my name.
Then Mum came in and woke me up
And spoiled my greatest game.

Andrew Collett

Goal!

Dad sat in his deckchair and snored.

But he jumped in the air when I scored.

The ball bounced off the shed

Hitting him on the head.

'What do you think you're doing?' he roared.

Derek Stuart

Dad's Goal Celebrations

When Dad scored a goal in the garden,
He celebrated with glee.
He put his T-shirt over his head
And ran into the tree.

So, when he scored his second,
He should have had more sense.
He tried to slide but couldn't stop
And smashed the garden fence.

And when he scored his third goal
He tried to hug my sister.
He slipped and tripped. His trousers ripped.
He fell on his face and missed her.

Paul Cookson

Batty Books

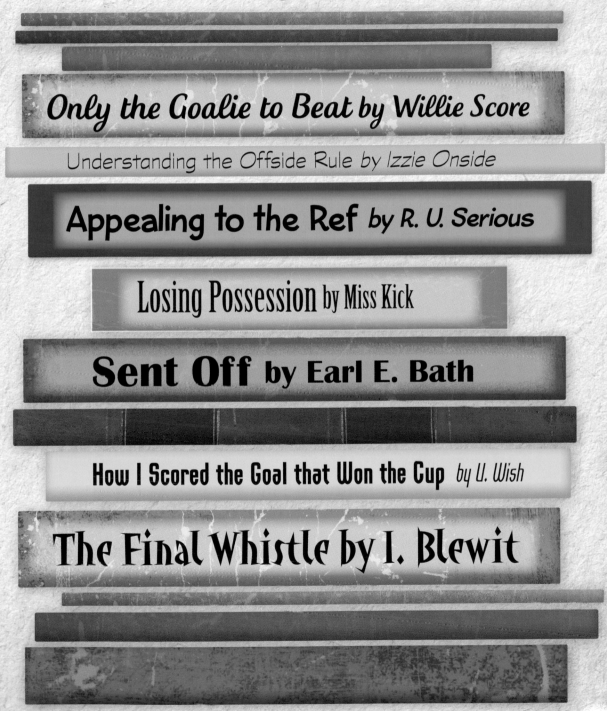

Only the Goalie to Beat by Willie Score

Understanding the Offside Rule by Izzie Onside

Appealing to the Ref by R. U. Serious

Losing Possession by Miss Kick

Sent Off by Earl E. Bath

How I Scored the Goal that Won the Cup by U. Wish

The Final Whistle by I. Blewit

The Dinosaur Rap

Come on everybody, shake a claw.
Let's hear you bellow, let's hear you roar.
Let's hear you thump and clump and clap.
Come and join in. Do the dinosaur rap.

There's a young T-rex over by the door
Who's already stamped a hole in the floor.
There's a whirling, twirling apatosaurus
Encouraging everyone to join in the chorus.

Come on everybody, shake a claw.
Let's hear you bellow, let's hear you roar.
Let's hear you thump and clump and clap.
Come and join in. Do the dinosaur rap.

There's a stegosaurus rattling his spines
And iguanodon making thumbs-up signs.
There's an allosaurus giving a shout
As he thrashes and lashes his tail about.

Come on everybody, shake a claw.
Let's hear you bellow, let's hear you roar.
Let's hear you thump and clump and clap.
Come and join in. Do the dinosaur rap.

John Foster

TYRANNY IS THE ONLY OPTION
VOTE T-REX

MIGHT IS RIGHT
VOTE T-REX

When the Dinosaurs Hold an Election

When the dinosaurs hold an election
There is never any debate.
T-rex is elected president.
He's the only candidate.

Simon Sharples

T-REX RULES

DOWN WITH DEMOCRACY
T-REX FOR PRESIDENT

For Your Safety's Sake
Vote T-rex

VOTE T-REX OR ELSE!

Terrified? You should be!
Vote T-rex

Why the Dinosaurs Died Out

The Earth started spinning at
a furious pace
And all of the dinosaurs were
flung into space.

Evie Lewis

If a Dinosaur Came to your House

If a dinosaur came to your house,
would you:
- invite him in for tea?
- offer him a seat on the settee?
- sit next to him and watch TV?
- flee?

John Foster

How do you know there's a dinosaur in the fridge?

You can't shut the door.

How do you know there's a dinosaur under your bed?

Your nose is touching the ceiling.

Why do dinosaurs like to eat snowmen?

Because they melt in their mouths.

Why did the dinosaurs eat raw meat?

They didn't know how to cook.

What do you give a dinosaur who's being sick?

Plenty of room.

Slick Nick's Dog's Tricks

Slick Nick's dog does tricks.

The tricks Nick's dog does are slick.

He picks up sticks, stands on bricks,

Nick's finger clicks, the dog barks SIX!

Slick Nick's dog does tricks

then gives Slick Nick sloppy licks.

Mick and Rick's dog's not so quick –
kicks the bricks, drops the sticks,
can't bark to six, is in a fix.
When Mick's or Rick's fingers click,
it wags its tail, gives sloppy licks.
Mick and Rick's dog doesn't do tricks.

But Slick Nick's dog does tricks.
The tricks Nick's dog does are slick.

David Harmer

Our Dog

Our dog chases kids on skates,
he does it every day
and if he doesn't stop it soon,
I'll take his skates away.

Larry O'Loughlin

Attention Dog Owners:

No dogs on
Nature Trails.
Thank you.

Attention Dogs:

Grrr. Bark. Woof.
Good dog.

For Sale: Dog
Eats
anything.

Especially fond
of children.

A Wizard's Apprentice
Called Jack

A wizard's apprentice called Jack,
Who had not quite mastered the knack
Of using the transforming pack,
Changed into a toad,
But was squashed on a road,
Before he could change himself back.

Pam Johnson

Oh, that's not a good sign.

BAD

Brainless

When they took an X-ray of the monster's brain,
The monster was in despair.
For the doctor said, shaking his head,
'I can't see anything there.'

Erica Stewart

About John Foster

I grew up in Carlisle and dreamed of
playing football for Carlisle United,
but they showed no interest in signing me. After
working as a firefighter in Canada, I became a teacher.
That's when I started to write poems and edit poetry
books. I've written about 1,500 poems and compiled over
100 anthologies. But none of them have been as much fun
as compiling the Chucklers anthologies.

I've chuckled over the silly signs, giggled at the
rapping dinosaurs, got my tongue in a twist trying to
say 'Slick Nick's Dog's Tricks', and have been reminded
of my dad pretending to be Bobby Charlton by 'Dad's
Goal Celebrations'.